THE SECRET ART OF SELF-CARE

PRACTICING WELLBEING AND RESILIENCE

DR. JAGADEESH PILLAI

|| Dedicated to all wisdom seekers around the World ||

Contents

Contents

PRAYER

**"Om Bhadram Karnebhih Shrunuyaama
DevaahBhadram Pashyemaakshabhiryajatraah
SthirairangaistushtuvaamsastanoobhihVyashema
Devahitam YadaayuhSwasti Na Indro
VridhashravaahSwasti Nah Pooshaa
VishwavedaahSwasti Nastaarkshyo ArishtanemihSwasti
No Brihaspatir DadhaatuOm Shantih, Shantih, Shantih"**

The literal meaning of this mantra is: OM. O Gods! Let us
hear auspicious words from our ears. O reverent Gods! Let
us behold propitious visions from our eyes, let our organs
and body be stable, healthy, and strong. Let us do that
which is pleasing to the gods in the life span allotted to us.
May Indra, inscribed in the scriptures, bring us fortune!
May Pushan, the knower of the world, grant us prosperity!
May Trakshya, who vanquishes enemies, bestow us with
blessings! May Brihaspati bring us success!
OM Peace, Peace, Peace.

About The Author

Dr. Jagadeesh Pillai is a renowned Guinness World Record holder, writer, and researcher hailing from Varanasi, also known as the abode of Lord Shiva. With a Ph.D. in Vedic Science and a range of creative ideas and achievements, he is a true polymath. He is the author of more than 100 books including Research Publications. Although his roots can be traced back to Kerala, the people of Varanasi hold him in high regard and affectionately consider him one of their own.

In 1998, Dr. Pillai was offered a job at Banaras Hindu University, but he left the position after only two months to pursue greater goals in life. He believed that in order to study Indian scriptures and engage in other creative endeavours, he needed to retire from the daily grind of working solely for money at a young age.

He started an export business from scratch, using the knowledge he had gained from a previous job in the industry. His intelligence and unique approach to business led to great success in a short period of time, earning him more in just a decade and a half than he would have in a lifetime working in a government job. Upon the passing of Dr. APJ Abdul Kalam, Dr. Pillai decided to leave the business and dedicate himself to reading, studying, researching, and experimenting.

During his tenure in the export business, Dr. Pillai traveled to over 16 countries, gaining valuable insight and experiencing the world and life in detail.

Dr. Pillai has achieved four Guinness World Records in the following subjects:

"Script to Screen" - In this record, Dr. Pillai produced and directed an animation film within the shortest time possible, breaking the previous record set by Canadians. He has also received numerous national and international awards and recognitions for this achievement.

Longest Line of Postcards - For this record, Dr. Pillai created a line of 16,300 postcards on the occasion of the 163rd anniversary of Indian Postal Day. The event also included a questionnaire about the Indian flag.

Largest Poster Awareness Campaign - Dr. Pillai designed an awareness campaign on the subject of "Beti Bachao - Beti Padhao" (Save the Girl Child - Educate the Girl Child) to achieve this record.

Largest Envelope - In tribute to the Indian Prime Minister's "Make in India" initiative, Dr. Pillai created a 4000 square meter envelope using waste paper to achieve this record.

Attempted - **70000 Candles on a 210 kg Cake** - To celebrate the 70th Indian Independence Day, Dr. Pillai attempted to light 70,000 candles on a 210 kg cake, which was recorded in World Records India.

Attempted - **Documentary on Dhamek Stupa of Sarnath in 17 Languages** - Dr. Pillai attempted to create a documentary on the Dhamek Stupa of Sarnath, dubbing it in 17 different languages. The result of this attempt is currently awaiting confirmation from the Guinness World Records.

Dr. Pillai is skilled in teaching the Bhagavad Gita, a Hindu scripture, and is popular among young people. He has helped many young people improve their lives through his motivational teachings.

In addition to teaching, he has composed and sung numerous Sanskrit Bhajans and patriotic songs.

He has also written and directed several short films and documentaries for awareness campaigns, and has volunteered with the police in both UP and Kerala to spread awareness about various issues through videos and photography.

Incredibly, he has produced and directed over 100 documentaries about the city of Varanasi, all on his own.

He has also helped and guided more than 25 boys and girls to achieve world records through creative and innovative methods. He is a multifaceted person who uses his intellect and the blessings given to him by God to excel in various areas. He is both a teacher and a student, always learning and teaching, and is able to master any subject he comes across.

He is a selfless social activist and motivational speaker who has overcome struggles and failures to become a successful and enthusiastic individual with a rich life experience.

In addition to his work with the Bhagavad Gita, he is also an efficient Tarot card reader, Astro-Vastu consultant, and a talented singer and composer. He has sung the entire Ram Charita Manas and Bhagavad Gita in his own compositions, and has sung the phrase "Lokah Samastha Sukhino Bhavantu" in 50 different languages. He is currently working on a detailed and scientific study of Vedas, Upanishads, Puranas, and the Bhagavad Gita. He has also composed and sung the Hanuman Chalisa and Gayatri Mantra in 108 and 1008 different compositions, respectively.

Awards - Four Times Guinness World Records, Winner of Mahatma Gandhi Vishwa Shanti Puraskar, Mahatma Gandhi Global Peace Ambassador, Kashi Ratna Award, Dr. APJ Abdul Kalam Motivational Person of the Year 2017, Mother Teresa Award, Indira Gandhi Priyadarshini Award, Bharat Vikas Ratna Award, Udyog Ratna Award, Vigyan Prasar Award, Poorvanchal Ratn Samman.

PREFACE

Self-care is often thought of as a luxury or a treat, but it is in fact a critical aspect of overall wellbeing and resilience. In today's fast-paced and demanding world, it is easy to become overwhelmed and to neglect our own needs, but doing so can have serious consequences for our physical and mental health, and for our ability to cope with life's challenges.

The Secret Art of Self-Care is a comprehensive guide to the importance of self-care, and provides practical and effective strategies for incorporating self-care into your daily routine. The book explores the role of mindfulness, self-compassion, managing perfectionism, coping with trauma, and the role of sleep and nutrition in self-care, and provides tools and techniques for developing the skills and habits needed to maintain physical and mental health, and build resilience in the face of life's challenges.

Self-care is not a one-time event, but a lifelong journey, and this book is designed to be a companion and a resource on that journey. Whether you are just beginning to explore the importance of self-care, or are looking to deepen your existing practices, The Secret Art of Self-Care offers practical guidance and inspiration to help you develop the skills and habits needed to thrive and flourish.

In this book, you will find a wealth of practical and actionable advice, as well as inspiring stories and case studies of individuals who have incorporated self-care into their daily lives, and who have reaped the benefits of improved physical and mental health, increased resilience, and greater overall wellbeing.

Whether you are looking to improve your physical and mental health, or to build resilience and thrive in the face of life's challenges, The Secret Art of Self-Care provides a roadmap to help you achieve your goals and live a life filled with meaning, purpose, and joy. So join us on this journey, and discover the Secret Art of Self-Care.

I

Art of Self-Care and its Importance for Wellbeing and Resilience

Self-care is a vital aspect of our lives that is often overlooked or neglected in our fast-paced, demanding world. It involves taking intentional steps to care for our physical, emotional, and mental health, so that we can live our lives to the fullest. The secret art of self-care is a skill that, when mastered, can help us build resilience, improve our wellbeing, and achieve greater happiness and fulfillment.

Self-care is not just about pampering ourselves with spa treatments or eating healthy foods. It is a holistic approach to life that encompasses all aspects of our lives and requires us to be intentional and proactive in our efforts to maintain balance and harmony. Self-care is not a one-time event but rather a consistent practice that requires time, effort, and dedication.

The Importance of Self-Care for Wellbeing and Resilience

Self-care is essential for our overall wellbeing and resilience, as it helps us manage stress, build resilience, and maintain a positive outlook on life. When we engage in self-care practices, we are better equipped to handle the challenges and stressors that come our way, as we have taken the time to nourish ourselves and build up our physical, emotional, and mental reserves. This, in turn, helps us approach life with a greater sense of calm, clarity, and purpose.

In addition to improving our resilience, self-care also helps us build a strong foundation for our overall wellbeing. It allows us to prioritize our physical and mental health, which in turn enables us to be more productive and motivated in other areas of our lives. When we are well-rested, nourished, and in a positive frame of mind, we are better equipped to tackle the tasks and responsibilities that come our way.

Moreover, self-care is a crucial aspect of our mental health, as it helps us manage feelings of anxiety, depression, and other mental health conditions. It enables us to develop coping skills and strategies for dealing with stress and difficult emotions, and helps us maintain a positive outlook on life. By taking care of ourselves and prioritizing our wellbeing, we are better equipped to handle the ups and downs of life with grace and resilience.

The secret art of self-care is a vital aspect of our lives that should not be overlooked. By taking intentional steps to care for our physical, emotional, and mental health, we can build resilience, improve our wellbeing, and achieve greater happiness and fulfillment. Self-care is a consistent practice that requires time, effort, and dedication, but the benefits it brings to our lives are well worth the investment. By making self-care a priority, we can live our lives to the fullest and enjoy all that life has to offer.

"Self-care is not selfish, it is essential for
maintaining your mental and physical
wellbeing."

Now that you have a better understanding of the importance of self-care for your wellbeing and resilience, it's time to start setting self-care goals and creating a plan for achieving them. Self-care goals can range from simple, daily habits to larger, long-term goals, but the key is to start somewhere and make self-care a priority in your life. In this chapter, we will discuss how to set self-care goals and create a plan that works for you.

Step 1: Identify Your Needs

The first step in setting self-care goals and creating a plan is to identify your needs. Take a moment to reflect on your physical, emotional, and mental health and consider what areas of your life you would like to focus on. Some common areas to focus on include exercise, healthy eating, stress management, relationships, and personal growth.

Step 2: Set Realistic and Achievable Goals

Once you have identified your needs, it's time to set self-care goals. When setting goals, it's important to be realistic and achievable. For example, if you haven't exercised in years, it may not be realistic to start with a daily, hour-long workout. Instead, start with a smaller, more achievable goal, such as a daily 10-minute walk. As you make progress and build momentum, you can gradually increase the intensity and duration of your workouts.

Step 3: Create a Plan

Now that you have set your self-care goals, it's time to create a plan. A self-care plan should include specific actions you can take to achieve your goals, as well as a timeline for when you would like to achieve them. For example, if one of your self-care goals is to exercise regularly, your plan might include setting aside time for a daily walk or workout, and creating a schedule for when you will do these activities.

Step 4: Track Your Progress

Tracking your progress is an important part of your self-care plan. It helps you stay motivated, see your progress, and make any necessary adjustments to your plan along the way. There are many ways to track your progress, including keeping a journal, using a self-care app, or setting up reminders on your phone.

Step 5: Celebrate Your Successes

Finally, it's important to celebrate your successes and recognize the progress you have made. Celebrating your successes will help you stay motivated and continue to make self-care a priority in your life. Whether it's a small win, such as cooking a healthy meal, or a larger accomplishment, such as completing a 10k race, take the time to acknowledge and celebrate your success.

Setting self-care goals and creating a plan is an important step in making self-care a priority in your life. By identifying your needs, setting realistic and achievable goals, creating a plan, tracking your progress, and celebrating your successes, you can improve your wellbeing, build resilience, and achieve greater happiness and fulfillment. Remember, self-care is a journey, not a destination, and it requires time, effort, and dedication. But with the right approach and mindset, you can master the secret art of self-care and live your life with Wellbeing and Resilience.

"The greatest gift you can give yourself is the gift of self-care."

ॐ

III

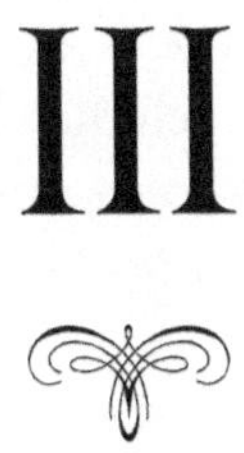

Self-care is an essential aspect of overall wellbeing and resilience, and developing a daily routine can help to ensure that you prioritize your own needs and create a supportive environment for yourself. Whether you are starting from scratch or simply looking to refine your existing routine, there are several steps you can take to build a routine that works for you.

Step 1: Identify Your Needs

The first step in building a self-care routine is to identify your specific needs. What do you need to feel good physically, emotionally, and mentally? This may include getting enough sleep, eating a nutritious diet, engaging in regular exercise, and taking time to relax and recharge. Consider keeping a journal to help you identify patterns in your physical, emotional, and mental state, and use this information to guide your self-care routine.

Step 2: Make a Plan

Once you have identified your needs, the next step is to

make a plan for how to meet them. This may include setting specific goals for each aspect of your self-care routine, such as aiming to get eight hours of sleep each night or to exercise for 30 minutes each day. Be realistic and flexible, as your needs may change over time, and don't be afraid to make adjustments as needed.

Step 3: Prioritize Self-Care in Your Daily Routine

Integrating self-care into your daily routine is crucial in order to make it a habit. This may mean setting aside specific times each day for self-care activities, such as starting your day with a morning meditation or taking a break in the middle of the day to stretch or go for a walk. Make sure to prioritize self-care activities, and don't let other tasks or obligations take priority.

Step 4: Create a Supportive Environment

Creating a supportive environment for yourself is an important part of building a successful self-care routine. This may include decluttering your living space, investing in comfortable and supportive sleepwear, and avoiding activities that are not conducive to self-care, such as working late into the night. Consider surrounding yourself with positive people who support your self-care routine and provide encouragement and motivation when needed.

Step 5: Be Patient and Consistent

Building a self-care routine takes time and patience, and it is important to be consistent in your approach. Try not to be too hard on yourself if you slip up, and remember that building a routine is a process that may take some time to perfect. Stick with it, and you will soon find that self-care becomes an integral part of your daily routine.

Self-care is essential to overall wellbeing and resilience, and building a daily routine can help you prioritize your needs and create a supportive environment for yourself. By identifying your needs, making a plan, prioritizing self-care in your daily routine, creating a supportive environment, and being patient and consistent, you can build a routine that works for you and supports your journey to a happier, healthier life.

"Mindfulness and self-compassion are key ingredients in the secret art of self-care."

৩

IV

Stress and emotions can be a significant source of difficulty in our daily lives, and learning to manage them effectively is an important aspect of self-care and overall wellbeing. When left unchecked, stress and negative emotions can lead to physical and mental health problems, and interfere with our ability to function effectively in daily life. Fortunately, there are several strategies that can help us to better manage stress and emotions and maintain our wellbeing.

Step 1: Identifying Triggers

The first step in managing stress and emotions is to identify the triggers that cause them. Triggers can be anything from a difficult conversation with a co-worker to a major life change, and they can vary greatly from person to person. Once you have identified your triggers, you can begin to develop strategies to manage them more effectively.

Step 2: Developing Coping Mechanisms

Developing coping mechanisms is an important part of

managing stress and emotions. Coping mechanisms are activities or strategies that help you to deal with stress and negative emotions in a healthy way. Examples of coping mechanisms include exercise, meditation, journaling, deep breathing, and talking to a trusted friend. It is important to experiment with different coping mechanisms to find the ones that work best for you.

Step 3: Practicing Mindfulness

Mindfulness is a powerful tool for managing stress and emotions, and it involves paying attention to the present moment without judgment. This can help to reduce feelings of stress and anxiety, and promote a sense of calm and inner peace. There are many different mindfulness techniques that you can try, such as meditation, deep breathing, and yoga. Make time to practice mindfulness regularly, and allow yourself to be fully present in the moment.

Step 4: Seeking Professional Help

If you find that stress and emotions are significantly impacting your daily life, it may be beneficial to seek professional help. A therapist or counselor can provide you with tools and strategies to manage stress and emotions more effectively, and help you to develop a personalized self-care plan. In some cases, medication may also be necessary, and a mental health professional can help you to make an informed decision about the best course of action for your individual needs.

Step 5: Building Resilience

Building resilience is an important aspect of managing stress and emotions, and it involves developing the ability to bounce back from difficult situations and maintain your wellbeing. Resilience can be built through regular self-care practices, such as exercise, mindfulness, and developing a supportive network of friends and family. By building resilience, you can become better equipped to handle stress and negative emotions, and maintain your wellbeing even in the face of adversity.

Managing stress and emotions is an important aspect of self-care and overall wellbeing. By identifying triggers, developing coping mechanisms, practicing mindfulness, seeking professional help, and building resilience, you can develop the tools and strategies you need to effectively manage stress and emotions and maintain your wellbeing. Remember, it is a journey, and it is important to be patient and persistent in your efforts to achieve a happier, healthier life.

*"Your health is your wealth, invest in it
through the practice of self-care."*

৪৩

Burnout is a state of emotional, physical, and mental exhaustion caused by prolonged stress and overwork. It can be a significant source of difficulty for individuals who are struggling to balance the demands of work, personal life, and other responsibilities. Burnout can lead to feelings of frustration, hopelessness, and detachment from work, and it can also have serious negative impacts on physical and mental health. Understanding and managing burnout is an important aspect of self-care and overall wellbeing.

Step 1: Recognizing the Signs of Burnout

The first step in managing burnout is to recognize the signs and symptoms. Common signs of burnout include feelings of emotional exhaustion, detachment from work, decreased satisfaction and accomplishment, increased cynicism and negativity, and physical symptoms such as fatigue, headaches, and insomnia. If you are experiencing these symptoms, it is important to take action to address the cause of your burnout.

Step 2: Identifying the Causes of Burnout

Burnout can be caused by a number of factors, including work overload, lack of control, unclear job expectations, and poor work-life balance. It is important to identify the specific causes of your burnout so that you can develop effective strategies for managing it. This may involve making changes to your work environment, such as reducing your workload or seeking more control over your responsibilities, or it may involve making changes to your personal life, such as developing better self-care habits or seeking support from friends and family.

Step 3: Developing a Self-Care Plan

Developing a self-care plan is a critical step in managing burnout. A self-care plan should include a variety of activities and habits that promote physical, emotional, and mental wellbeing. Examples of self-care activities include exercise, mindfulness, spending time with loved ones, and engaging in hobbies and interests. It is important to make self-care a priority, and to make time for it every day, even when you are feeling busy or stressed.

Step 4: Seeking Support

Seeking support is an important aspect of managing burnout. Talking to a trusted friend, family member, or therapist can help you to better understand and manage your stress and emotions. You may also benefit from seeking support from coworkers or joining a support group, as this can help you to feel less isolated and more connected to others.

Step 5: Building Resilience

Building resilience is an important aspect of managing burnout, and it involves developing the ability to bounce back from difficult situations and maintain your wellbeing. Resilience can be built through regular self-care practices, such as exercise, mindfulness, and developing a supportive network of friends and family. By building resilience, you can become better equipped to handle stress and negative emotions, and maintain your wellbeing even in the face of adversity.

Understanding and managing burnout is an important aspect of self-care and overall wellbeing. By recognizing the signs of burnout, identifying its causes, developing a self-care plan, seeking support, and building resilience, you can develop the tools and strategies you need to effectively manage burnout and maintain your wellbeing. Remember, it is a journey, and it is important to be patient and persistent in your efforts to achieve a happier, healthier life.

*"Self-care is the foundation of resilience,
build it every day."*

❧

VI

Resilience refers to the ability to bounce back from adversity and maintain a positive outlook, even in the face of stress, challenge, and change. Building resilience is an important aspect of self-care and overall wellbeing, as it enables individuals to better handle stress and negative emotions, and to maintain their health and happiness even in the face of adversity.

Step 1: Understanding the Benefits of Resilience

The first step in building resilience is to understand the benefits of resilience and why it is important for self-care and overall wellbeing. Resilience can help individuals to better handle stress, negative emotions, and change, and to maintain their health and happiness even in the face of adversity. Additionally, resilience can help individuals to build stronger relationships, improve their performance at work and in other areas of life, and increase their overall sense of wellbeing.

Step 2: Building Physical Resilience

Physical resilience involves taking care of your physical health and wellbeing, and building the strength and endurance to handle physical stress and challenges. To build physical resilience, it is important to engage in regular physical activity, such as exercise, and to eat a healthy, balanced diet. Additionally, it is important to get enough sleep and to manage stress through techniques such as deep breathing, progressive muscle relaxation, and mindfulness.

Step 3: Building Mental Resilience

Mental resilience involves developing the ability to handle stress and negative emotions, and to maintain a positive outlook even in the face of adversity. To build mental resilience, it is important to engage in regular self-care practices, such as exercise, mindfulness, and spending time with loved ones. Additionally, it is important to seek support from others when needed, and to build strong relationships with friends, family, and coworkers.

Step 4: Challenging Negative Thoughts and Emotions

One of the key aspects of building mental resilience is challenging negative thoughts and emotions. Negative thoughts and emotions, such as anxiety, fear, and anger, can be detrimental to our wellbeing and can prevent us from effectively handling stress and adversity. To challenge these negative thoughts and emotions, it is important to practice mindfulness and to engage in positive self-talk, such as focusing on your strengths and abilities, and finding ways to reframe negative thoughts and emotions in a more positive light.

Step 5: Building a Supportive Network

Building a supportive network of friends, family, and coworkers is another important aspect of building resilience. A supportive network can provide a source of comfort and support during difficult times, and can help individuals to better handle stress and negative emotions. Additionally, building a supportive network can help individuals to develop a sense of connection and belonging, and to build stronger relationships with others.

Step 6: Engaging in Positive Activities

Engaging in positive activities, such as hobbies and interests, can also help individuals to build resilience. Positive activities can help to reduce stress and negative emotions, and to increase feelings of happiness and wellbeing. Additionally, engaging in positive activities can help individuals to build new skills, explore new interests, and meet new people, which can further support their resilience and overall wellbeing.

Building mental and physical resilience is an important aspect of self-care and overall wellbeing. By understanding the benefits of resilience, building physical and mental resilience, challenging negative thoughts and emotions, building a supportive network, and engaging in positive activities, individuals can develop the tools and strategies they need to effectively handle stress, negative emotions, and adversity, and to maintain their health and happiness even in the face of challenges. Remember, building resilience is a journey, and it is important to be patient and persistent in your efforts to achieve greater wellbeing and happiness.

"It's not about pampering yourself, it's about taking care of yourself."

ɞ

Positive thinking and gratitude are powerful tools that can help individuals to improve their mental and emotional wellbeing, and to build resilience in the face of stress, challenge, and change. These skills can help individuals to maintain a positive outlook, to cultivate happiness and contentment, and to develop a greater sense of meaning and purpose in life.

Step 1: Understanding the Benefits of Positive Thinking

The first step in harnessing the power of positive thinking is to understand the benefits of positive thinking. Positive thinking has been shown to have a range of benefits for mental and emotional wellbeing, including reduced stress and anxiety, improved mood, and increased feelings of happiness and contentment. Additionally, positive thinking has been linked to better health outcomes, including lower blood pressure and reduced risk of depression and anxiety disorders.

Step 2: Practicing Positive Thinking

Practicing positive thinking involves actively focusing on positive thoughts, emotions, and experiences, and minimizing negative thoughts and emotions. To practice positive thinking, individuals can engage in techniques such as positive self-talk, visualization, and mindfulness, and they can seek out positive experiences and interactions with others. Additionally, individuals can practice gratitude, which is another powerful tool for improving mental and emotional wellbeing.

Step 3: The Benefits of Gratitude

Gratitude involves focusing on the things in life that we are thankful for, and recognizing the good things in our lives, even in the face of adversity. The practice of gratitude has been shown to have a range of benefits for mental and emotional wellbeing, including increased happiness, reduced stress and anxiety, and improved mood. Additionally, gratitude has been linked to stronger relationships and a greater sense of meaning and purpose in life.

Step 4: Practicing Gratitude

Practicing gratitude involves actively focusing on the things in life that we are thankful for, and recognizing the good things in our lives, even in the face of adversity. To practice gratitude, individuals can engage in techniques such as keeping a gratitude journal, focusing on positive experiences, and expressing gratitude to others. Additionally, individuals can practice mindfulness, which can help them to focus on the present moment and to cultivate greater awareness and appreciation for the things in life that bring them joy and contentment.

Step 5: Building Positive Habits

Building positive habits is an important aspect of harnessing the power of positive thinking and gratitude. Positive habits, such as engaging in physical activity, eating a healthy, balanced diet, and spending time with loved ones, can help individuals to maintain a positive outlook and to cultivate happiness and contentment. Additionally, positive habits can help individuals to build resilience, and to better handle stress and negative emotions.

Step 6: Seeking Support

Seeking support from others can also be an important aspect of harnessing the power of positive thinking and gratitude. Support from friends, family, and loved ones can help individuals to maintain a positive outlook and to build resilience, and it can also provide a source of comfort and support during difficult times. Additionally, seeking support can help individuals to build stronger relationships, and to develop a greater sense of meaning and purpose in life.

Positive thinking and gratitude are powerful tools that can help individuals to improve their mental and emotional wellbeing, and to build resilience in the face of stress, challenge, and change. By understanding the benefits of positive thinking and gratitude, practicing these skills, and forming positive habits, individuals can cultivate greater happiness, contentment, and meaning in their lives. It is essential to be patient and consistent in your efforts to tap into the power of positive thinking and gratitude, as these skills require time and dedication to master. However, with patience and persistence, you can reap the many rewards of these invaluable tools.

"Sleep, nutrition, and exercise are the pillars of self-care and overall wellbeing."

છ

Building support systems and connecting with others is an essential aspect of self-care and can play a critical role in promoting mental and emotional wellbeing and resilience. Whether it is through close relationships with family and friends, supportive communities, or professional networks, having a strong support system can provide individuals with a sense of security, comfort, and encouragement in the face of life's challenges.

Step 1: Building Relationships with Family and Friends

The first step in building a strong support system is to focus on close relationships with family and friends. These relationships can provide individuals with a sense of connection, support, and understanding, and they can play a critical role in promoting mental and emotional wellbeing. To build and strengthen relationships with family and friends, individuals can engage in activities such as spending time together, sharing experiences, and being there for one another during difficult times.

Step 2: Joining Communities and Social Groups

Joining communities and social groups can also be an important aspect of building a strong support system. These groups can provide individuals with a sense of belonging and connection, and they can also provide a source of support, encouragement, and understanding. Examples of communities and social groups include religious organizations, hobby groups, and social clubs. Joining these groups can help individuals to build relationships with others who share similar interests and experiences, and to connect with individuals who can provide support and understanding.

Step 3: Building Professional Networks

Building professional networks can also be an important aspect of building a strong support system. Professional networks can provide individuals with a sense of connection, support, and encouragement in the workplace, and they can also play a critical role in promoting career success and fulfillment. To build professional networks, individuals can attend networking events, join professional organizations, and seek out mentorship and coaching relationships.

Step 4: Seeking Help When Needed

Seeking help when needed is also an important aspect of building a strong support system. Whether it is through therapy, counseling, or other forms of support, seeking help can provide individuals with the tools and resources they need to address mental and emotional challenges, and to promote wellbeing and resilience. It is important to seek help when needed, and to not be afraid to ask for support from family, friends, communities, and professional networks.

Step 5: Cultivating Empathy and Compassion

Cultivating empathy and compassion is also an important aspect of building a strong support system. Empathy and compassion involve understanding and relating to the feelings and experiences of others, and they can play a critical role in promoting strong relationships and a sense of connection. To cultivate empathy and compassion, individuals can engage in practices such as mindfulness, self-reflection, and active listening, and they can also seek out opportunities to give back to others and to help those in need.

Step 6: Maintaining Strong Relationships

Maintaining strong relationships is an ongoing aspect of building a strong support system. Whether it is through regular communication, shared experiences, or simply being there for one another, maintaining strong relationships is essential to ensuring that a support system remains strong and effective. It is important to be intentional and proactive in maintaining strong relationships, and to seek out opportunities to deepen connections and build trust with family, friends, communities, and professional networks.

Building support systems and connecting with others is an

essential aspect of self-care, and it can play a critical role in promoting mental and emotional wellbeing and resilience. By building relationships with family and friends, joining communities and social groups, building professional networks, seeking help when needed, cultivating empathy and compassion, and maintaining strong relationships, individuals can cultivate a strong support system that provides a sense of security, comfort, and encouragement.

"Managing perfectionism and coping with trauma are crucial aspects of self-care."

ରଓ

IX

Finding and pursuing one's passions is a critical aspect of self-care and can play a crucial role in promoting mental and emotional wellbeing and resilience. Having a sense of purpose and fulfillment, and engaging in activities that bring joy and meaning to one's life, can help individuals to feel more fulfilled, motivated, and engaged in their daily lives. In this chapter, we will explore how individuals can find and pursue their passions, and how this can promote wellbeing and resilience.

Step 1: Identifying Your Passions

The first step in finding and pursuing your passions is to identify what you are passionate about. This can be a difficult and often a time-consuming process, but it is essential to figuring out what brings meaning and fulfillment to your life. Some individuals already have a clear idea of what their passions are, while others may need to explore and experiment to figure out what they are passionate about.

To help identify your passions, it can be useful to reflect on your interests, hobbies, and values. What activities do you enjoy doing in your free time? What do you value in life? What are your strengths and abilities? Answering these questions can help to provide insight into what you are passionate about, and can help to guide you in your search for your passions.

Step 2: Exploring Your Passions

Once you have identified your passions, the next step is to explore them further. This can involve trying new activities, taking classes or workshops, or seeking out opportunities to learn more about your passions. It is important to be open and flexible in your exploration, and to not be afraid to step outside of your comfort zone.

Step 3: Incorporating Your Passions into Your Daily Life

Once you have explored your passions and found those that bring joy and fulfillment to your life, the next step is to incorporate them into your daily life. This can involve making time for your passions, and finding ways to integrate them into your daily routine. Whether it is through hobbies, volunteer work, or professional pursuits, incorporating your passions into your daily life can help to bring meaning and purpose to your life, and can help to promote wellbeing and resilience.

Step 4: Staying Committed to Your Passions

Staying committed to your passions is an ongoing aspect of finding and pursuing them. Whether it is through regular engagement in activities related to your passions, or by setting and pursuing goals related to your passions, staying committed to your passions is essential to ensuring that they remain a meaningful and fulfilling aspect of your life.

Step 5: Balancing Your Passions with Other Areas of Your Life

Balancing your passions with other areas of your life is also an important aspect of finding and pursuing your passions. Whether it is through work, family, or other commitments, it is essential to find balance and to not let your passions consume your life. Finding balance can involve setting boundaries, prioritizing your time, and seeking support and encouragement from others.

Finding and pursuing your passions is a critical aspect of self-care, and it can play a crucial role in promoting mental and emotional wellbeing and resilience. By identifying your passions, exploring them, incorporating them into your daily life, staying committed to them, and balancing them with other areas of your life, individuals can cultivate a sense of purpose and fulfillment, and can promote wellbeing and resilience in their daily lives.

"The secret art of self-care is about finding
balance and harmony in your life."

℗

X

Perfectionism is a complex trait that is often viewed as desirable and admirable. It is the drive to strive for excellence, achieve high standards, and avoid mistakes. However, perfectionism can also be harmful to one's mental and emotional wellbeing if not managed correctly. This chapter will explore the nature of perfectionism, its negative effects, and strategies for managing it effectively.

What is Perfectionism?

Perfectionism is a personality trait characterized by a relentless drive for excellence, an unrelenting pursuit of high standards, and a fear of making mistakes. Perfectionists have a strong internal pressure to perform perfectly, and they often judge their self-worth based on their achievements. They believe that their performance reflects who they are as a person, and that their value is tied to their ability to achieve.

Perfectionism comes in two forms: adaptive and

maladaptive.

Adaptive perfectionism is a healthy form of perfectionism that motivates individuals to work hard and strive for excellence. Adaptive perfectionists are able to set high standards for themselves, but they are also able to recognize their limitations and accept that they may not always be able to meet their goals. In contrast, maladaptive perfectionism is characterized by an unhealthy and rigid pursuit of perfection. Maladaptive perfectionists have an unrealistic and unrelenting need to perform perfectly, and they are often unable to accept their limitations or acknowledge their mistakes.

The Negative Effects of Perfectionism While perfectionism can be motivating and lead to high achievement, it can also have negative effects on one's mental and emotional wellbeing. Research has shown that perfectionism is associated with a range of mental health problems, including anxiety, depression, and burnout. Perfectionists are often their own harshest critic, and they may engage in self-criticism and negative self-talk. They may also avoid taking risks and trying new things out of fear of making mistakes, which can limit their opportunities for growth and development.

In addition, perfectionism can also affect relationships. Perfectionists may have difficulty accepting feedback and criticism, and they may struggle to form close and meaningful relationships. They may also be perceived as rigid or inflexible, which can make it difficult for others to connect with them.

Strategies for Managing Perfectionism Managing perfectionism requires a multi-faceted approach that involves changing one's beliefs, habits, and behaviors. Some strategies for managing perfectionism include:

Changing perfectionist beliefs:

It is important to challenge the belief that perfectionism is a desirable trait and that mistakes are unacceptable. Perfectionists need to recognize that it is okay to make mistakes, and that they are not their mistakes. They should also learn to appreciate their efforts and accomplishments, rather than focusing solely on the outcomes.

Setting realistic goals: Perfectionists should set goals that are achievable and realistic. They should also recognize that there is a difference between striving for excellence and being perfect. By setting realistic goals, perfectionists can reduce the pressure they put on themselves to perform perfectly.

Practicing self-compassion: Perfectionists should practice self-compassion and treat themselves with kindness and understanding. They should learn to accept their limitations and acknowledge their mistakes, and they should avoid self-criticism and negative self-talk.

Engaging in self-care: Perfectionists should engage in self-care activities, such as exercise, meditation, and hobbies, to reduce stress and improve their mental and emotional wellbeing.

Seeking support: Perfectionists may benefit from seeking support from friends, family, or a mental health professional. Talking to others about their experiences can help perfectionists to gain perspective and learn new strategies for managing their perfectionism.

Celebrating small victories: Perfectionists should learn to celebrate their small victories and accomplishments, rather than focusing solely on the end goal. By recognizing their progress and celebrating their successes, perfectionists can reduce the pressure they put on themselves and increase their motivation to keep moving forward.

Practicing self-forgiveness: Perfectionists should learn to forgive themselves for their mistakes and failures. They should recognize that making mistakes is a natural part of the learning process, and that they can learn from their experiences and grow from them.

Perfectionism is a complex trait that can have both positive and negative effects on one's mental and emotional wellbeing. However, by changing perfectionist beliefs, setting realistic goals, practicing self-compassion and self-care, seeking support, celebrating small victories, and practicing self-forgiveness, perfectionists can effectively manage their perfectionism and improve their overall wellbeing.

The above strategies are not a quick-fix solution, but rather a long-term process of learning and growth. By embracing imperfection and learning to accept their limitations, perfectionists can increase their resilience and lead a happier, more fulfilling life.

ॐ

"Be gentle with yourself, self-care is a journey
not a destination."

ೞ

XI

Self-compassion is an important aspect of self-care and is crucial for overall wellbeing. It refers to the ability to treat oneself with kindness, understanding, and compassion, especially in difficult situations or when faced with personal failures. This chapter will explore the concept of self-compassion, its benefits, and practical strategies for building self-compassion in daily life.

What is Self-Compassion?

Self-compassion is a mindset that involves treating oneself with kindness, understanding, and compassion, especially in difficult situations or when faced with personal failures. It involves recognizing that everyone makes mistakes and experiences difficult emotions, and that it is important to be gentle and understanding with oneself in these situations.

Self-compassion has three components: self-kindness, common humanity, and mindfulness. Self-kindness refers to the ability to treat oneself with kindness and understanding, rather than with harsh self-criticism. Common humanity involves recognizing that everyone experiences difficult emotions and setbacks, and that these experiences are a normal part of the human experience. Mindfulness involves being present in the moment and acknowledging one's thoughts and emotions without judgment.

Benefits of Self-Compassion Research has shown that self-compassion is associated with a range of positive outcomes, including:

Reduced stress and anxiety: Self-compassion can help to reduce stress and anxiety by providing a supportive and understanding inner voice, which can help to manage difficult emotions and thoughts.

Improved mental health: Self-compassion has been shown to be associated with better mental health outcomes, including lower levels of depression and higher levels of wellbeing.

Increased resilience: Self-compassion can help build resilience by providing a supportive and understanding inner voice, which can help to manage difficult emotions and thoughts in the face of adversity.

Improved self-esteem: Self-compassion can lead to improved self-esteem by reducing the harsh self-criticism that many people experience, and by providing a more supportive and understanding view of oneself.

Enhanced relationships: Self-compassion can also enhance relationships by reducing interpersonal conflict and improving communication and understanding.

Building Self-Compassion Building self-compassion is a process that involves learning new ways of thinking and behaving, and requires regular practice and effort. Here are some practical strategies for building self-compassion:

Practice mindfulness: Mindfulness is an important component of self-compassion, and can help to increase self-awareness and reduce self-criticism. Practicing mindfulness can involve activities such as meditation, journaling, or simply taking a few deep breaths and paying attention to one's thoughts and emotions.

Speak to yourself kindly: Self-compassion involves speaking to oneself in a kind and understanding way, rather than with harsh self-criticism. This may involve using kind and encouraging words, focusing on one's strengths and accomplishments, and reminding oneself of common humanity.

Practice self-care: Self-care is an important aspect of self-compassion, and involves taking care of one's physical, emotional, and mental health. This can include activities such as exercise, good nutrition, and engaging in leisure activities that bring joy and relaxation.

Seek support: Reaching out to trusted friends and family, or seeking professional support from a therapist, can help to build self-compassion by providing a safe and supportive environment for exploring one's thoughts and emotions.

Reframe negative thoughts: Self-compassion also involves reframing negative thoughts and beliefs about oneself, and replacing them with more supportive and understanding ones. This may involve challenging negative beliefs and replacing them with evidence that supports a more positive view of oneself.

Self-compassion is an important aspect of self-care and wellbeing, and is associated with a range of positive outcomes. By practicing mindfulness, speaking to oneself kindly, engaging in self-care, seeking support, and reframing negative thoughts, anyone can build self-compassion and enhance their overall wellbeing.

"By taking care of yourself, you are better
equipped to care for others."

℘

XII

Mindfulness is a powerful tool that can be used to promote self-care and wellbeing. It is a state of being present and fully engaged in the moment, without judgment or distraction. This chapter will explore the role of mindfulness in self-care, its benefits, and practical strategies for incorporating mindfulness into daily life.

What is Mindfulness?

Mindfulness is a state of being present and fully engaged in the moment, without judgment or distraction. It involves paying attention to one's thoughts, emotions, and sensations in a non-judgmental and accepting way, and can help to increase self-awareness and reduce stress and anxiety

Benefits of Mindfulness Research has shown that mindfulness is associated with a range of positive outcomes, including:

Reduced stress and anxiety: Mindfulness has been shown to be effective in reducing stress and anxiety, and can help to manage difficult emotions and thoughts.

Improved mental health: Mindfulness has been shown to be associated with better mental health outcomes, including lower levels of depression and higher levels of wellbeing.

Increased resilience: Mindfulness can help to build resilience by providing a supportive and understanding inner voice, which can help to manage difficult emotions and thoughts in the face of adversity.

Improved focus and productivity: Mindfulness can also improve focus and productivity by reducing distractions and increasing the ability to stay focused and engaged in tasks.

Enhanced relationships: Mindfulness can also enhance relationships by reducing interpersonal conflict and improving communication and understanding.

Incorporating Mindfulness into Daily Life Incorporating mindfulness into daily life is a process that requires regular practice and effort. Here are some practical strategies for incorporating mindfulness into daily life:

Practice mindfulness meditation: Mindfulness meditation is a simple and effective way to cultivate mindfulness, and involves focusing on the breath and being present in the moment. It can be practiced for just a few minutes a day, and can be done anywhere, at any time.

Engage in mindful activities: Engaging in activities that require full attention, such as yoga, gardening, or cooking, can help to cultivate mindfulness and increase self-awareness.

Pay attention to thoughts and emotions: Paying attention to one's thoughts and emotions in a non-judgmental and accepting way can help to increase self-awareness and reduce stress and anxiety.

Practice self-compassion: Practicing self-compassion is an important aspect of mindfulness, and involves treating oneself with kindness, understanding, and compassion, especially in difficult situations or when faced with personal failures.

Engage in mindful breathing: Engaging in mindful breathing, such as taking a few deep breaths, can help to reduce stress and increase focus and clarity in the moment.

Mindfulness is a powerful tool that can be used to promote self-care and wellbeing. By incorporating mindfulness into daily life through activities such as mindfulness meditation, engaging in mindful activities, paying attention to thoughts and emotions, practicing self-compassion, and engaging in mindful breathing, anyone can cultivate mindfulness and enhance their overall wellbeing.

"Self-care is not about being perfect, it's about
being kind to yourself."

ജ

XIII

Understanding and Managing Trauma

Trauma is a deeply distressing or disturbing experience that can have a profound impact on an individual's mental and emotional health. This chapter will explore the definition of trauma, its causes, the effects of trauma on mental and emotional health, and strategies for managing trauma in a healthy and effective way.

What is Trauma?

Trauma is a deeply distressing or disturbing experience that can have a profound impact on an individual's mental and emotional health. It can take many forms, including physical, emotional, or sexual abuse, natural disasters, or exposure to violence or conflict. Trauma can also be the result of a one-time event or a series of events that occur over a longer period of time.

Causes of Trauma Trauma can be caused by a wide range of events, including:

Physical, emotional, or sexual abuse: Physical, emotional, or sexual abuse can cause trauma, and can have a lasting impact on an individual's mental and emotional health.

Natural disasters: Natural disasters such as hurricanes, earthquakes, or floods can cause trauma, especially if the event results in injury, loss of property, or loss of life.

Exposure to violence or conflict: Exposure to violence or conflict, such as war or domestic violence, can cause trauma and have a lasting impact on mental and emotional health.

Medical procedures: Certain medical procedures, such as surgeries, can cause trauma, especially if they are particularly invasive or result in significant pain or injury.

Effects of Trauma on Mental and Emotional Health Trauma can have a profound impact on mental and emotional health, and can result in a range of symptoms, including:

Anxiety and fear: Trauma can result in anxiety and fear, and can cause individuals to feel constantly on edge or hyper-vigilant.

Depression: Trauma can result in depression, and can cause individuals to feel hopeless and helpless.

Post-Traumatic Stress Disorder (PTSD): Trauma can also result in Post-Traumatic Stress Disorder (PTSD), which is a mental health disorder that is characterized by intrusive thoughts, avoidance behaviors, and hyper-arousal.

Substance abuse: Trauma can result in substance abuse, as individuals may turn to drugs or alcohol to cope with the emotional pain and distress associated with trauma.

Self-harm: Trauma can result in self-harm, as individuals may engage in self-harming behaviors as a way of coping with the emotional pain and distress associated with trauma.

Strategies for Managing Trauma Managing trauma can be a difficult and complex process, but there are a number of strategies that can help individuals to cope and heal in a healthy and effective way. Some of these strategies include:

Seek support: Seeking support from a trusted friend, family member, or mental health professional can help individuals to cope with the emotional pain and distress associated with trauma.

Engage in therapy: Engaging in therapy, such as cognitive-behavioral therapy (CBT) or trauma-focused therapy, can help individuals to work through the traumatic experience and develop healthy coping mechanisms.

Practice self-care: Practicing self-care, such as engaging in physical activity, eating a healthy diet, and getting enough sleep, can help individuals to manage the physical and emotional impact of trauma.

Engage in mindfulness: Engaging in mindfulness

practices, such as mindfulness meditation, can help individuals to reduce stress and anxiety, and increase self-awareness and emotional regulation.

Seek help for substance abuse: If an individual is struggling with substance abuse as a result of trauma, it is important to seek help from a substance abuse treatment program. Treatment can help individuals to overcome their addiction, and provide support and resources for long-term recovery.

Build resilience: Building resilience can help individuals to better manage the impact of trauma, and recover from the effects of trauma in a healthy and effective way. This can be done by developing healthy coping mechanisms, developing strong relationships with others, and engaging in activities that promote physical and emotional wellbeing.

Seek out trauma-focused resources: There are a number of trauma-focused resources available, including support groups, online resources, and trauma-focused books and publications. Seeking out these resources can help individuals to better understand and manage the impact of trauma, and provide additional support and guidance as they work through the healing process.

Understanding and managing trauma is a critical aspect of self-care, and requires a multi-faceted approach that addresses both the physical and emotional impact of trauma. By seeking support, engaging in therapy, practicing self-care, and building resilience, individuals can work through the traumatic experience and develop healthy and effective coping mechanisms for long-term recovery.

"Remember, self-care is an investment in your future, so make it a priority."

ॐ

XIV

The Importance of Sleep and Nutrition for Self-Care

Self-care is a critical aspect of overall wellbeing and resilience, and it is essential to prioritize sleep and nutrition as part of a comprehensive self-care practice. Both sleep and nutrition play a vital role in maintaining physical and mental health, and are critical to overall wellbeing and resilience.

Sleep:

Importance of quality sleep: Quality sleep is essential for overall physical and mental health. When we sleep, our bodies have the opportunity to repair and regenerate, and our brains have the opportunity to process and consolidate information from the day.

Adequate sleep: Adequate sleep is important for overall health and wellbeing. The National Sleep Foundation recommends that adults get 7-9 hours of sleep per night, while teenagers and children require more.

Benefits of sleep: Getting adequate, quality sleep has a number of benefits, including improved memory, increased energy and productivity, and improved mood and emotional regulation.

Sleep hygiene: Sleep hygiene refers to the habits and practices that support healthy sleep. This can include developing a consistent sleep schedule, creating a sleep-conducive environment, avoiding screens before bedtime, and practicing relaxation techniques before bed.

Nutrition:

Importance of good nutrition: Good nutrition is essential for overall physical and mental health. The food we eat provides the nutrients and energy our bodies need to function optimally.

Nutrient-dense foods: Consuming nutrient-dense foods, such as fruits and vegetables, lean proteins, and whole grains, can help to support overall health and wellbeing.

Avoiding harmful foods: Avoiding foods that are high in sugar, salt, and unhealthy fats can help to maintain good physical and mental health.

Hydration: Hydration is also important for overall health and wellbeing. Adequate hydration can help to support physical performance, mental clarity, and overall wellbeing.

Sleep and nutrition are critical aspects of self-care, and are essential for maintaining physical and mental health, and promoting overall wellbeing and resilience. By prioritizing quality sleep and good nutrition, individuals can support their overall health and wellbeing, and build the resilience needed to face life's challenges.

"Be mindful, be compassionate, be resilient - this is the secret art of self-care."

❧

XV

Practicing Wellbeing and Resilience through the Secret Art of Self-Care

Self-care is a critical aspect of overall wellbeing and resilience, and is essential for maintaining physical and mental health, and for thriving in the face of life's challenges. This book has explored the importance of mindfulness, self-compassion, managing perfectionism, coping with trauma, and the role of sleep and nutrition in self-care.

The Secret Art of Self-Care involves taking time to focus on one's own needs and well-being, and to engage in practices and habits that promote overall health and wellbeing. This can include engaging in mindfulness practices, building self-compassion, managing perfectionism, coping with trauma, and prioritizing sleep and nutrition.

In order to make self-care a regular and effective part of your routine, it is important to approach it with an open mind, and to be mindful of your own needs and goals. This can involve setting aside time each day to engage in self-care practices, and finding ways to incorporate self-care into your daily routine.

It is also important to be patient and compassionate with yourself, and to approach self-care with kindness and understanding. This can involve letting go of perfectionistic tendencies, and recognizing that self-care is a lifelong journey, with ups and downs along the way.

Ultimately, the Secret Art of Self-Care is about taking care of yourself, and developing the skills and habits needed to maintain physical and mental health, and build resilience in the face of life's challenges. By engaging in self-care practices, individuals can develop the skills and resources needed to thrive and flourish, and to live a life filled with meaning, purpose, and joy.

"The best way to find yourself is to lose yourself in the practice of self-care."

❧

OTHER BOOKS OF THE AUTHOR

1.   The Moments When I Met God
2.   Kashiyile Theertha Pathangal
3.   Guru Gyan Vani
4.   Abhiprerak Gita
5.   Assi Se Jain Ghat Tak
6.   Hopelessness Of Arjuna
7.   The Soul And It's True Nature
8.   Sense Of Action (Karma)
9.   Action Through Wisdom
10.   Action Through Wisdom
11.   Theory And Practical Of Every Action
12.   Logical Understanding Of The Supreme
13.   The Imperishable Supreme
14.   Yatra Nishadraj Se Hanuman Ghat Tak
15.   Yatra Karnatak Ghat Se Raja Ghat Tak
16.   Yatra Pandey Ghat Se Prayagraj Ghat Tak
17.   Yatra Ranjendra Prasad Ghat Se Dattatreya Ghat Tak
18.   Yaatrasindhiya Ghat Se Gwaliar Ghat Tak
19.   Yatra Mangala Gauri Ghat Se Hanuman Gadhi Ghat Tak
20.   Yatra Gaay Ghat Se Nishad Ghat Tak
21.   Maa Ganga, Ghaten Evm Utsav
22.   Ganga Arti Dev Deepavali Evam Any Utsav
23.   Potentials Of Digitalized India
24.   Vedic Consciousness
25.   A Brief Introduction To Vedic Science
26.   Kashi Ke Barah Jyotirling
27.   Impact Of Motivation
28.   Let's Have A Milky Way Journey
29.   Color Therapy In A Nutshell

59. The Holistic Cow: A Look At The Physical, Spiritual, And Cultural Importance Of Cows In India
60. Arts Of Healing
61. Exploring The Divine
62. Understanding Five Elements
63. The Etymology Of Ram
64. Symbols Of India
65. Voice Of Change (About Speeches Of Great Men)
66. She Speaks (About Speeches Of Great Women)
67. Patriotism On Celluloid – Brief About Patriotic Films
68. The Music Of Motivation: A Brief Guide To Inspirational Film Songs
69. Unlocking The Secrets of The Dashopanishads
70. A Cultural Mosaic
71. Ancient Traditions, Modern Minds
72. Ecos Of Ancient Wisdom
73. Beneath The Surface
74. From Temples To Ashrams
75. Sages Of The Subcontinent
76. The Art Of Healling (Ayurveda, Yoga & Naturopathy)
77. Indian Kitchen
78. The Festivals Of India
79. The Indian Epics Retold
80. The Power Of Mantras
81. The Indian River Ganges
82. The Indian Architecture
83. Rites Of Passage
84. The Indian Silk Road
85. The Indian Literature
86. The Indian Villages
87. The Indian Folks & Crafts
88. The Way Of Buddha
89. The Ramayan Of Tulsidas

Contact

DR. JAGADEESH PILLAI

MBA & PhD in Vedic Science

Four Times Guinness World Record Holder

Winner of Mahatma Gandhi Vishwa Shanti Puraskar and
Global Peace Ambassador

Gemology, Astro & Vastu Consultant - Spiritual Counselor

Consultant for designing World Record Ideas

Efficient Tarot Card Reader

9839093003

myrichindia@gmail.com

drjagadeeshpillai@facebook

drjagadeeshpillai@instagram
jagadeeshpillai@youtube

www. JAGADEESHPILLAI.com

|| LOKAHA SAMASTHAHA SUKHINO BHAVANTU ||

౭౩